Bob

Thank you for
your friendship
+ your fine
service

Jimmy
Carter

Behind the News:

The Story of John C. Burke

Behind the News

The Story of John C. Burke

ROBERT GOODWIN

JLK2 PUBLISHING

Dedicated to Steve & Marla.

CONTENTS

Behind the News:

The Story of John C. Burke

CHAPTER ONE

Introduction

How does one measure a man when two people first meet? First impressions they say are some of the most important. It lays the foundation for everything that follows. This is an introduction to this book unlike most. It is not an introduction to the book itself but a chance to delve into what it was like to first meet Finney Burke. It is one of those rare, once in a lifetime meetings....

Too often we find amongst us great individuals who spend a lifetime toiling away at a particular job that helps shape our lives. Then one day those individuals disappear and we are left with a void. Life moves forward, but so much information on the history of what has happened is lost to the next generation forever once these silent but great individuals pass on. The word impressive cannot be used enough to describe someone who, from a very young age, realizes what they want to do in life and then they go out and do it. This is such an amazingly rare feat. Most people today rush through life and to have four or even five careers in a lifetime is no longer rare. Life continues to spiral at an ever increasing pace. Technology has connected the world in such a way as to make many things obsolete. Yet some things have stayed much the same with only minor changes.

Growing up I had a friend who loved trees. In fact there were not too many days in a given summer where I would not find my friend either up or around some great massive oak or laurel. He would spend countless hours milling about the forests behind his house; building tree forts, talking to birds, and just getting lost in his own made up world. He grew up to become an arborist. He knew from such a young age what he wanted to do and who he wanted to be. As I grew older I began to appreciate him more and more. I spent many hours wondering if I would ever meet anyone else in my life like him. Could there actually be someone else out there who, from such a young age, knew what he wanted out of life?

Contrary to my friend, my whole life has been spent running from project to project and job to job. In fact, this is how most of us live out our days. We find a job, do it for a while and then, POOF...we move on. Better money, a chance for travel, a desire for change, or even boredom, leads us all in new directions. My friend did not have this problem and I envied him for it. What must it be like? To have your path laid out for you even before you realize it is truly unique.

As I grew older I came to realize just how unbelievable it is to love what you do so much from such a young age. It took me many years to finally find my "passion". I never thought I would meet someone like my friend again in this lifetime, until I met "Finney".

In 2012 I began working in a small hamlet, Magnolia Massachusetts as well as her larger neighbor Manchester. While there, I met quite a few "locals" who continually talked about one particular individual named "Finney" Burke. I would hear stories about what an interesting character Finney was and how he knew just about everything that had gone on in and around the North Shore since he had covered just about every news story over the past 50 years through various jobs in the news industry. I was told he was a colorful chap who, although reserved, had a knack for telling colorful stories. Many of these stories were embedded with quite a few of those now famous New England four letter words. I was quite astonished that no matter whom I met in Magnolia, they all seemed to know "Finney".

As time wore on, I was approached by a couple of people who thought that I should write a book about the life of Finney and through his story also help tell about the changes that have taken place in and around Magnolia and Manchester over the past half century. While the project intrigued me on many levels, I was apprehensive at first. One of the biggest problems each generation faces is the loss of information when the previous generation passes on. As an ethnographer and writer I know the importance of capturing even the smallest of details that for some may seem insignificant. As generations change, having information from the past can really help make sound decisions about the future. It was this idea that began to make me wonder if this person "Finney" might be an untapped resource of information and I continued to muse over the possibility of writing the book.

It is never easy to put someone's life down on paper. The responsibility can be overwhelming. On the one hand you want to share the entire breadth of information that encompasses the life of that particular individual, yet on the other hand you want to make sure to respect the wishes of the person you are writing about. Especially when that particular person is a writer as well. The result lends to the ages old question of " What do I write about?"

Writing a biography can also bring up a whole host of other issues. It is not like creative writing where you can pick up a pen and dabble a few incoherent sentences and then come back to it weeks or months later and pick up where you left off or even change the story all together. In a biography, the story has already been written. Also with a biography, the writer becomes the keeper of all the important information on someone's life, the good, the bad, AND the ugly. This is where it becomes painfully important to make sure as a writer that you are up to the challenge.

As a result, I definitely took my time in assessing whether or not I wanted to carry the burden of telling someone's life story, especially someone like Finney. In short, for me writing this book or not was not an easy answer at first. Life always has a way of creeping up on us and I knew that writing Finney's story would need to be tackled with great dedication. A man like Finney deserved nothing less. So I was apprehensive about taking on such a large project having just completed a five-year project on another book. However after meeting Finney for the very first time I was hooked. It was not hard to fall into the trap, as I am sure you will undoubtedly see....

My wife and I first met Finney and his wife Irene at a restaurant along with Steve Martin and his lovely wife Marla. Steve and Marla are also residents of Magnolia and it was their original idea to write this book. They had previously met Irene and Finney many times and, as others before them, easily fell into the idea of wanting to get the story of Finney's life down on paper. Finney is that type of person. One of those larger than life characters that remains hidden behind a reserved outward appearance. Steve was the catalyst behind me finally saying yes to this fortuitous dinner (knowing full well that the power of Finney's story as well as his ability to draw someone in would take care of the rest). Even up until this point I remained apprehensive. Afraid is more like it. Having already heard so much about Finney from the locals, I was so worried about how I would possibly be able to put into words the life that was Finney Burke.

So there we all were…three couples sitting around a table, each wondering how the evening would turn out. However, it did not take long to realize that something unique was unfolding before my very eyes. What happened that evening was fantastic and sealed my fate; quickly intertwining my life with Finney's. Steve, being the consummate spokesman easily broke down the initial barriers that are present when people first meet. There is always apprehension when dealing with the unknown but Steve's solid ability to open the evening with smiles and a toast soon gave way to a sigh of relief for all as we began to chat in earnest.

Finney was quiet and reserved at first, as he is most often. Yet, there was a sparkle in his eyes. The kind of sparkle that makes everyone sit up straight and take notice. They say you can know a truly remarkable person just by looking into their eyes; eyes that have seen much; honest eyes. Finney was indeed an interesting individual and I was drawn into those eyes. It was like being on a boat in the middle of the ocean to look into his eyes. I found my mind swimming in those sea blue eyes and thinking of all that Finney had seen in his eighty-five years. Yes indeed there was definitely a story here to be sure.

His wife Irene on the other hand was much more open and talked freely about many things. She was lovely. My wife and her formed an instant bond and the stories flowed as easily as the wine. Irene had almost as many stories to tell as Finney. From her family in Portugal and the travels she had enjoyed to the restaurant business, which she had been a part of, Irene could definitely hold her own in a conversation and leave folks asking for more. These two people had seen and done much both together and apart and they embodied a soulful spirit. Looking at my face light up, it did not take long for both Steve and Marla to realize they had achieved the desired outcome.

As the evening continued to open up, so did Finney. His stories and colorful language albeit spoken in a gentle quiet tone, definitely persuaded me to truly commit myself to telling his whole story. Finney is the kind of person who does not need to speak loudly; in fact he doesn't. He commands your attention without ever having to raise his voice. My gut tells me he knows full well what he is doing with his softly spoken words. You cannot help but want to know more and I found myself leaning closer and closer to him as the night wore on. He draws you in. I've heard from many people now that he is so soft spoken that it is hard to always catch what he is saying. Some have blamed it on age. No, this is simply not true. Finney speaks softly and with that carefree sparkle he watches as you lean further in to hang on every word. He is the kind of person who understands the power of language. Each word is carefully thought over before it is uttered and thus, each word is important on its own. He is as sharp as a tack and he knows this. Even his stories are carefully crafted. Stories he has told countless times can seem as if he is telling them for the very first time.

Today, many of the younger generation talk before they think about the consequences of their words. The language has become inundated with new ways to say the same thing due to technology. Everything is shortened and acronyms have replaced so much. This is simply not so with Finney. He was brought up in a time when words carried much more meaning and thought was put into how to use them. For Finney, a man who made his living off of the use of words, thought precedes action. I suspect from a very young age, (although he would tell you differently if you ask him about his school work), Finney was drawn to words. He was very curious about many things, especially what was happening locally. News it would seem was of great interest to his young mind. The end result of all this, is a soft-spoken man with infinitely important things to say, and, who gives the listener a rare opportunity to learn; as long as they are willing to lean in. And in my case I could not help myself.

At the end of a very long evening we all shook hands and hugged and thus began our journey together. It is a journey that has covered many interviews and countless hours at the computer. My wife, bless her soul, has become a part of the process and my interviews with Finney have become more or less a get together amongst friends. Irene always makes sure to have plenty of sweets at the ready and it is fun watching Finney, with that ever present twinkle in his eye, sneak a third pastry while Irene is not looking and is busy in the kitchen. I suspect she knows full well what he is up to and makes it a point to scurry around just long enough so that he can "think" he is getting away with something.

As a writer, you cannot truly put into words what these moments mean. Sometimes just being able to sit back and watch Finney and Irene interact has given me great insight into who they are and what they stand for. They are quite a couple. As a person being asked to take on this project it has become quite an honor. It has allowed my wife and I to think about our own lives and how much more time we hope to be able to spend together. As a result of this endeavor I have also begun to think about how much interacting with other generations can give us in the form of information. The dissemination of information between different age groups carries great merit. We can, if we listen closely, learn about past mistakes, understand our history better, or quite simply enjoy making new friends across generational divides. In the case of Finney and Irene, it is all of the above...and this is their story.

CHAPTER TWO

A Brief Background on Magnolia

This book is not a historical account of the entire history of Magnolia and Manchester. That would undoubtedly be a daunting task and has been somewhat attempted before. However, it is important to place some emphasis on the years previous to Finney's arrival in order to get a better understanding of what forces helped to shape his formative years living in the area.

Both of the towns, located on the North Shore of Massachusetts, are interesting places. Towns? Yes, in this novel I will take the liberty of calling Magnolia a town! This seaside area is actually part of the city of Gloucester but it really has a town feel unto itself. It is not the legal papers or official seal that creates a town, it is the people. Village or town or hamlet, each of these places can spring up almost anywhere as long as there are good hearted citizens who bond together to create a place where folks feel safe and welcomed. As to this, Magnolia and Manchester are undoubtedly towns as much as Salem or Lynn. The area is a great mixture of "old salts", long standing families, newly settled suburbanites, and your occasional passer by. Lexington Avenue in Magnolia was once a center of great commerce and a large hotel in town catered to the rich and famous. Many large summer estates dotted the shoreline and money flowed. Great architects and landscape designers like Frederick Law Olmsted, created magnificent gardens behind rows of cast iron fences. During the summer months the enclave would swell with guests coming to visit the ocean retreat and enjoy the ever-present sea breezes that flowed off of the Atlantic. Even Finney and his wife Irene have a very intimate connection to Lexington Avenue as shall be shown.

Much of why Manchester and Magnolia became more popular and thus expanded upon came about from a variety of reasons. During the turn of the past century there was a massive shift in the way people thought about health. Prior to this, people in general were not as keenly aware of the benefits of fresh air and good exercise as well as better overall hygiene. In fact sickness was dealt with by closing people inside and the way many were taken care of only added to the overall maladies that plagued small towns like Manchester and Magnolia. The cemetery of today is riddled with people who died much to young during the 18th and 19th century. Diet and lack of medicine also added to the overall unhealthful spirit of the town.

But over time, new discoveries were made in medicine and health as the scientific community opened up and embraced new ideas. On a global level these ideas spawned a new way of helping to take care of people both from a personal as well as professional level. While this does not seem important to discuss in a biography about one person, it is in fact a very key part of Finney's story. At eighty-five years old, Finney came along at the very height of this medical change of thought and the newly improved way of thinking that most doctors and scientists were acting upon. This had a trickle down affect on the everyday citizen. Before this period of awakening, it was thought that fresh air carried the disease and thus, one way to stem the tide was to close up the shutters and lock the doors. While this seems rather silly now, it was put into practice in many homes right up through the depression and Finney's arrival.

But the late 1920's and early 1930's saw a paradigm shift in medical thinking. Even bathing regularly took on a more positive role in the family. Saturday night baths for the entire family were still common in most homes but overall the general public began to become more aware of the simple fact that bathing your fourth child in the same bathwater as your first on a given night did not always produce a healthy child. It was still not an easy task to heat the water and maneuver through large families on a Saturday evening in preparation for looking ones best for Sunday church. But, never the less, a more practical bathing and hygiene regimen began to take hold. So how did this shift affect places like Manchester and in kind Finney's early years?

Well it was during this time period that many physicians began to call for an increase in outdoor activities. Woman who prior to this, were generally precluded from many sports and most of the outdoor activities, could now enjoy themselves by taking nature walks, playing at the beach, and even participating in tennis. In fact the area of Manchester and Magnolia became so popular with the sport that a Davis Cup match was played in 1896 on clay courts located off of Ocean Avenue. These matches drew the eyes of the nation and the North Shore was soon the talk in places as far away as California. It never ceases to amaze me at how interconnected lives and places can be. Finney's family was a very well known one in Manchester but they had little contact with folks as far away as California during Finney's formative years. Yet, Manchester as a whole was just coming into its own. And Magnolia was soon to follow. The new shift in health consciousness and the desire for outdoor recreation and exercise drew people away from the hustle and bustle of the cities and a desire welled up to return to the smaller towns, especially those located by the seashore.

Leisure time, which in prior decades had only been enjoyed by a few, now became leisure time enjoyed by many. This had a direct impact on businesses as new ideas on how to cater to a growing population sprung forth. And with the ocean, front and center, in places dotted throughout the North Shore the destination was ripe for expansion.

The idea of free time spent wallowing along a beach, or taking a walk in a park, or even playing outdoor games as couples or with extended families was originally kept mostly to those with the means to take time away from the day to day grind of putting food on the table and raising a family. The wealthy families were the first to try this new leisure style and it caught on. Manchester and Magnolia quickly became destinations for relaxing. A brand new concept was born, Day Tripping. Of course these small "side" trips soon turned into much more. "Vacationing" became something more and more people talked about. And the outdoors and places that were surrounded by nature became choice destinations. In Manchester and Magnolia the area had everything people were looking for. While the area boasted some great views of the Atlantic Ocean, there were also plenty of wooded areas to explore. And, at this time the native wildlife was still pretty prevalent within a short buggy ride. The area also had a rich farming history and was incredibly picturesque. For those coming from the big city this was a wonderful opportunity to get back to an atmosphere that held a sense of natural wonderment.

This entire mode of thinking was a new concept in America. First it was experimented with as more and more families began to create a financial wealth that allowed them the time to commit to these activities. Yet, in America something else new and quite unique was taking shape. With the burgeoning of a newly formed middle class there was now time to partake in these new past times for many more than just the select wealthy people.

In England, lawn games became all the rage with commoners. Prior to this, most of these games and social gatherings were played and enjoyed among the royalty much like they were enjoyed among the wealthy in America. Now however, people had more expendable time on their hands and the attraction to these new games caught on. This had a singular affect on the people living back in America. What was the "in" thing in England usually became a sensation here in America and lawn games were no exception. Yet one other major addition came about as a result of a new burgeoning middle class; badminton and especially croquet allowed both woman and men to participate in social activities together. The Victorian era for all of its "stuffiness" was actually a time when woman truly began to move towards more independence. This independence also coincided with a change in appearance. Clothing and style adapted with the times as well and new stores sprung up to cater to the needs of those who had money to spend. Even in small cities like Beverly and Gloucester, new shops opened and new items could be bought from over seas.

In the 1920's this had a direct impact on Magnolia and Manchester. The Oceanside Hotel located just off of Lexington Avenue had taken shape in years past. Yet now, with the influx of people who had both time and money, the hotel became a more central economic player in the development of the area. The hotel continued to grow in prominence as early Hollywood discovered the benefits of vacationing in the area. This love affair with Magnolia would continue for many years. Many movie stars would make it a point to book their vacations at the Oceanside Hotel during the summer months. This obviously added jobs to the surrounding community members not to mention adding to the social fabric of the town as a whole. The movie stars of yesteryear mingled socially with the local people who called Manchester and Magnolia home. It was very unlike today with regard to the famous movie stars. The beach of course was a huge draw, as was the opportunity to just get away from the filming industry and work. However, the movie industry also saw opportunity on the North Shore and many films from the 1920's through to the outbreak of WWII were actually produced in the area.

As a result of all this, the cottages lining Shore Road grew into stunning mansions as the elite Hollywood actors decided to build summer homes. But these were in fact only a handful. It was the large business owners from Boston who really began to buy up land in Magnolia and the surrounding areas to build their dream homes. These homes were serviced by an ever-increasing number of immigrants who continued to stream northwards from Boston in search of work after arriving in the country. Irish, Italian, and Scottish workers came in droves and many of these individuals settled down in the area and had families of their own. These newly formed close knit families added to the changing patchwork of small social enclaves that only helped to make Magnolia a truly colorful place. So many different European cultures melded together to create the social fabric that made up these two small towns. Each social unit added to the value of the area and many adopted different cultural norms from each other as a result. This undoubtedly created a new set of cultural norms that became embedded by the time Finney came along. Most folks by that time had created a pretty set standard in the town. The infrastructure was in place, most of the families were well established, and generations had come and gone. Yet there was even then, a continual stream of new people who melded into the landscape.

The sea as stated earlier also added a backdrop to the way people lived their lives. The roughly hewn beachheads and rocky slopes that jutted out into the foreboding and sometimes angry ocean, were a juxtaposition to the inhabitants themselves. The folks that called this area home were tough; you had to be. Fishing had long been established in Gloucester and it was, up until the early twentieth century, a major fishing port. Even today, the industry survives but it has grown to be an incredibly challenging lifestyle for those who still ply the trade. The difficulties are mainly economic. However there is still, even today, the inherent danger of working on the ocean. Years ago this danger was even more profound. The lack of technology and weather forecasting along with the types of sailing vessels themselves, created an industry that had a direct impact on many woman. The fisherman who set sail to gather large catches in hopes of creating wealth for their families always took their lives into the hands of Davy Jones. Many of these fishermen called Magnolia and Manchester home. Yet even more widows could be found amongst the inhabitants. The seas claimed so many good men over the first few centuries of the founding of this great nation and many towns are filled with the graves to prove it. Manchester and Magnolia are no exception. And, even in Finney's day the sea continued to take its toll.

While most of the immigrants who came from Boston after arriving in America found work on the large estates which continued to be built up around the area, or even in local labor positions such as the laundry services or construction, some did make their way onto the large fleet of fishing vessels that called Gloucester home. As stated, the local cemeteries are dotted with the names of many who were lost at sea and never made it back to the shores of Magnolia but it was the wives left behind who created yet another new phenomenon. In the past, sickness, war, or even a job accident would create a widow; now whole communities might have to deal with the loss of many in a single moment. The widows left behind would need to be cared for and this also added to the strength of the community. Magnolia and Manchester had strong bonds between neighbors. Each cared for the other. In a small New England community this was paramount to the success of everyone.

But, for all the influx of various groups of people, new money, and an increase in overall different social norms than had been previously practiced farming still controlled a lot of the commerce in the area. Large farms spread out from areas right along the coastline and single-family steads pushed all the way into the hinterland of surrounding communities. Some of these farms were massive and employed large numbers of the local inhabitants. The farms stretched throughout Manchester and Beverly and well into areas that sometimes encompassed hundreds and even into thousands of acres. Dotted along these farmsteads rose the large estates that grew to dominate certain parts of the landscape from the 1860's onward. In New England and even in Manchester and Magnolia the families who owned these massive farm estates became central figures in town politics and in other business ventures as well.

With the end of the Civil War came a resurgence of American economic might and a boon such as the country had never seen began to take shape. Names like Crane, Rooosevelt, Coolidge, R.B. Williams, George Carter, John Wilkins, and families like the Thornton's and Butler's, to name a few, had many acres as part of their estates and utilized the land in various farming and animal husbandry businesses while at the same time leaving large open tracts for natural recreation. It was the writings of John Muir that began to form a new way of thinking for the people who held onto these massive tracts of land. This all culminated in 1889 with the opening of Yosemite National Park. Yet again, a seemingly unrelated national situation would affect two small areas 3000 miles away. People's eyes were turned outwards towards nature.

Manifest Destiny and the idea that we could control nature changed to a more holistic idea of becoming one with nature.

Olmsted had created the idea of parks and built Central Park in New York as his model. He then went on to build landscapes all around the nation including right in Manchester and Magnolia. The idea of nature and parks and the outdoors created an opportunity for the larger land-owners to create habitat for the local wildlife. All of this heralded in the idea of building parks on the community level which led to a direct affect on Finney's childhood and love of sports; one sport in particular which I will get into more in later chapters... baseball.

During the dawn of the new century, nature even took a front seat in the way people viewed their own lives. Doctors purported the health benefits of being out in nature and people gravitated towards this new line of thought. The birth of landscape design and implementation gave rise to even more luxurious estates along the shores of Magnolia and Manchester. Olmsted's work on these estates was a harbinger for even more economic growth in the area since the building of these landscapes created many job opportunities. The Chicago Worlds fair and Frederick Law Olmsted's creations of New York's Central Park only added to the desire to sculpt the nature surrounding these large houses. For the two towns, the new push toward landscaping created yet another economic vehicle for inhabitants to not only gain employment but use the money they were paid to help support other industries. The Coolidge family alone, who owned a large estate along the coast and held various other pieces of land throughout Magnolia and Manchester at one time, employed over 50 individuals. Many of the wealthy families did not just own one piece of property but in fact owned a number of fields that stretched away from the water for many miles. The jobs were plenty and everyone benefited. In later years some of this land was sold off to various companies and the state as highway route 128 was slowly built up.

All of these different socio and economic groups who were brought together in such a small area of land definitely added to the already growing discrepancy between the have and have not's. While the middle class was indeed growing, the wealthy individuals who now called the area home were also gaining in a continually spiraling upwards of monetary wealth. The result could be felt up and down the eastern Massachusetts shoreline. Social thought changed and morphed as it undoubtedly does in any town where people are separated by economics. Some people used disposable income, what in prior centuries had been unheard of, on how to decide where money was allocated, what goods were to be purchased and what jobs could be created. The idea of consumerism, as we now know it, was born and continuing to heat up. The boom of this was occurring during Finney's youth. After the much-maligned Great Depression that saw the Nation's wealth halved, folks were now beginning to realize the worst was indeed behind them. The area saw growth from President Roosevelt's New Deal that was a direct result of thinkers like Carnegie, Muir and Olmsted, and it helped to usher in prosperity once more. This new wealth helped to fund increases for business in Manchester and Magnolia including everything from the local markets to specific storefronts that catered exclusively to people of means. The results only added to the fuel of a burgeoning business center in Magnolia as well as storefronts along Magnolia's water front district as more and more stores and restaurants continued to open up to serve an ever growing demand. The same could be said for its neighbor Manchester.

As more and more families from the city settled into summer homes along the shores, the pressure to keep up with the news heralded in the local newspaper business on a much larger scale. Multiple newspaper companies sprung up from Beverly to Gloucester and all vied for the attention of the people. And, on the North Shore, there were plenty of news stories to fill the pages. Newsprint also gave yet another opportunity for young people to make a dollar as deliveries increased as will become evident in young Finney's life.

Yet, by no means did the entire area forego the industries that originally shaped the fabric of both towns. Regardless of how many new stores opened, or how many new industries were developed as a result of increased capital, Magnolia especially, never lost the ability to feel like a sleepy little New England village. In later years as the area continued to develop with new hotels and restaurants, one could step away from a place like the Oceanside Hotel and walk down from Lexington Avenue back towards the open pastures and the area still felt slow and unhurried. It was this Magnolia and Manchester that Finney grew up in. The area was such a unique blend of big city business people, famous actors, and just everyday inhabitants that worked the land or worked in service sectors to earn a wage.

This feeling of a quiet community can still be felt throughout many small towns in New England including both Magnolia and Manchester even today. And for the residents the feeling is something to cherish. This is what draws folks from such far away places to visit. Even back at the turn of the last century, though many different people from many varied backgrounds now called Magnolia home, the sense of community only grew stronger. That sense of community, in the face of such varying socio-economic factors really made this area unique. But as in any situation where different people come together, certain entities help in shaping cohesion.

The church was a major focal point that helped to bridge this gap between the different socio and economic classes that were prevalent in both towns and also helped to keep that feeling of town unity. Sunday services brought the estate owners into town where they mixed with local small-scale farmers, storefront owners, newspaper delivery boys, and restaurant purveyors. The Mass services at the church were held at 7AM, 9AM, and again at 10:30AM. Religion played an integral role in the society even more so than today. The church was a gathering place and a time when local folks could get news from each other on the well being of others. Regardless of what social group you belonged to, religion was a large part of how your family raised you, how and when you interacted with others in the community, and in some cases, it even played a key role in your livelihood. While for many, Sundays were a time of worship and a day where a person rested from the toils of work, for others, the gathering at church was a moment when the large families would come together and undoubtedly discuss matters of interest. Sunday was also a very busy time for the newspaper industry, as we shall see in later chapters.

Sundays ushered in a time for large family dinners and, in the summer time, a chance to take a ride into the countryside if one had the opportunity to do so. Horse and Buggies dotted the landscape until Henry Ford changed everything. At the Oceanside Hotel, Sundays were reserved for pleasant relaxation after a night of dancing at the weekly cotillion that was held in the main dance hall. This tradition began in the early 1870's as the nation rebuilt following the Civil War. Many of the current ideas over social activities, most of which were taking place in Victorian England at the time, trickled across the pond and made their way into mainstream America like the lawn games. But other ideas surfaced as well. From fashion, to sports, and even the subtle ways in which the opposite sexes mingled, permeated the small towns and hamlets like Magnolia and Manchester. And, with the Oceanside Hotel as a backdrop, the "regular" folk got a first hand taste of what it was like to socialize in this manner. Dance styles became more numerous and some were even down right risqué and whether it was people working the dance or attending, these styles and ideas found their ways into the homes locally. Charades became a massive hit and many dinner parties at the larger mansions had charade games as a focal piece of entertainment.

Overall for its size, Magnolia was indeed a place rich in social tapestry. Many towns throughout New England displayed the same qualities. As new families and immigrants settled in the area, each individual left an indelible mark on the place. Magnolia was like a mini melting pot with a lot to offer during her heyday.

It is important to remember that all of these social events, a new push toward leisure activities, shopping, and hotels were not enjoyed by everyone although most did in fact benefit. The goal of this chapter is to give a broad view of all that was happening in and around Magnolia during the turn of the past century. Yes there was plenty of money and large estates that dotted the land. But that money was held by the few not the many. Businessmen did come from the city to vacation near the beach and by the nineteen twenties Hollywood had discovered the area as was discussed prior. Yet fishermen still plied their wares. Blacksmiths were still needed to shoe horses. And farming was still a major industry.

Some of the largest farms on the North Shore were found in the open areas between Magnolia and Ipswich. Some of the largest families like the Appleton's held vast land over the interior. However even within reach of the coastline there were some very large farms that produced everything from dairy products and eggs to vegetables for mass consumption. Barnard Stanwood, the Fuller family, Everett Cressy and The Wilkins family to name a few, all made their living off of the land. The industry employed many of the other local families in town as well. Vast farms such as these needed a heavy dose of skilled labor in order to succeed. But these jobs did not pay very well and although the work was indeed steady, the workers were continually held back from making great economic strides.

One other facet of the town that slowly brought about social change, an overall chance of economic success, and a steady flow of news was the train. This industry like no other changed the entire fabric of society on both a large and small scale. The railroad was the king of change. The Boston and Maine railroad (B and M) passed right through the town of Manchester on its way up and down the coastline and as such, it was like an artery pumping the area full of life daily. The train did not just create an opportunity for people to come and visit Manchester and Magnolia. The train was a bridge that residents could use to branch out and find work elsewhere like in Boston. In fact the train itself was a tool of employment for some who called Manchester home including Finney's own father. And it was the railroad that brought the national news in the form of print. Newsprint was instrumental in helping to keep all the residents of Magnolia in tune with what was going on in the greater world. Without the train and the information and connectivity that it relayed, Magnolia might not have become as vibrant a place as it had certainly become by 1930. The train took fathers away from the family and into the city for work. Yet again, the train added another spoke in a constantly moving wheel that helped to continually change the social fabric of the area. Where before, men needed to find work on an incredibly local level, now they could hop on a train and find new types of employment. The city also brought about a chance to make more money with better wages, which in turn led to an increase in disposable income not just for the wealthy but also for those who had previously not been able to spend on the extra items that were in such demand.

Local storefronts definitely benefited from the train service in Magnolia. Goods flowed in and out of town via the train and there was definitely an overall shift in the type of goods sold. Items slowly became more exotic and people had an opportunity to purchase goods that previously had not been available. Farming equipment and tools used for various jobs were also sold alongside imported goods from Europe. For all of New England's uniqueness in design and style, Victorian England rubbed off on even the most frugal of families. Stained glass windows, velvet upholstery, and a new fad-the Knick Knack became normal sights inside of family homes. In short, people began to collect things in large quantities. Objects moved from those which one needed to those which one desired.

The mixture of all of the different styles, various jobs, and array of colorful cultures seen with the influx of immigrants, truly made for an interesting place. Magnolia for all its smallness in size was rather large in stature. True, there were far larger towns up and down the coast and many of them were going through the same interesting developments as Magnolia. However, given the land area that Magnolia covered and the relative social and economic complexity that was evident, it could be argued that Magnolia was in some ways unique. With the massive Oceanside Hotel, the wealthy families whose homes dotted the landscape, the train that rambled through on its way North, and the incredible array of immigrant workers all rolled into a very small area, Magnolia was like a small mirror of how life must have been like in some of the much larger cities. Even in Manchester that was larger by area, much of this uniqueness was prevalent.

However, as with most small towns that see an economic and social boon, the ebb and flow of the engines that made it all possible at last began to falter. While the train engines still roared by going about the daily grind, another engine, the engine of prosperity was quickly being devoured by larger forces. As 1929 came to a close the nation was gripped in an economic battle. Banks were closing in record numbers, the stock market had crashed, and small towns were making runs on their own financial institutions for fear of having nothing left when the dust settled. By the time the great depression happened Magnolia's splendor, as with most towns, had indeed begun to wane.

Records indicate however, that Manchester in some ways remained vibrantly solvent although on a much smaller scale. Most of the large wealthy families who lived in the area were able to weather the crash of 1929 and many town businesses continued to produce and sell goods. Between 1929 and 1940, the town actually saw an increase in new businesses that was very rare during this time period. This anomaly was obviously not felt everywhere. But for Clifton Burke, having moved from Rowley to reside in Manchester prior to the crash of 29' in hindsight seems to have been a good move. Through thriftiness and the community coming together both Manchester and Magnolia came out of the depression in as good a shape as one could have hoped. But it was not easy. Much rationing of goods and new ideas on how to weather the economic storm were implemented.

The overall assent of the area towards financial prosperity had been slow and methodical. As a result, the area had grown and flourished over time. Folks had absorbed new ideas, new jobs and a new approach on social norms. They were in a better position now to absorb the national free fall that the crash was producing. The area boasted a sort of mini paradise by the sea. Folks could live and work there but also vacation there as well. Prior to the crash, as time went on and the assent continued, the wealth created gave the local population many opportunities to create businesses and provide for larger families. The natural elements with the stunning scenery and ocean views led the prosperous city dwellers to also settle in the area and over time all of the aforementioned variables led to the expansion of both Manchester and Magnolia.

While the crash of 1929 however was immediate and the results for Magnolia were felt instantly, the town due to the creativity and location it held should be commended for how it came through the 1930's. While Magnolia resembled Manchester in many ways, it was smaller and much of the economic stability was a direct result of living off its larger parent Gloucester. There was no slow and gradual demise of the area; there was only shock and awe as common families saw their wealth slip out of their fingers overnight. The largest difference between what occurred with the crash of 2008 and the crash of 1929 for Magnolia is clearly evident. In 1929 almost all of the families that lived in Magnolia counted upon local industry as a means. In 2008 with globalization, the town and many others like it were able to weather the storm far better. The Magnolia of 1929 marked a severe turning point for the town. Yet, like so many other small towns and hamlets, Magnolia and her residents were, if nothing else, resilient. The people of Manchester helped out as best they could. And those who called Magnolia home also found help from other surrounding communities. Yes, while it is true that the crash forever changed some of the ways in which business and commerce where done and in the way social norms were portrayed, the town persevered. In fact one could argue that in many ways Magnolia did not crash. There was just a shift to a new way of doing things- a paradigm shift as it were. Where the folks of Magnolia took on the downward spiral with vigor and found new ways to reshape the area. Like most periods of hard times, the citizens of Magnolia found strength in the simple. Family, friends, business partners and the church all played a significant role in reinventing Magnolia after 1929.

This reinvention began slowly just as the previous assent. It was during this time that the modern Magnolia we know today began to find roots in the soil and grow. Some of the previous splendor did indeed remain and make it through the crash. The Oceanside Hotel, while it most definitely lost a large clientele at first, did in fact survive. This was if nothing else, a testament to the fortitude of the people who called the area home. The Kershaw family bought the hotel in 1931. George Kershaw was in construction but with the crash he could not find work. He saw something in the old hotel though and purchased it. Working tirelessly he strove to continue the legacy and through hard effort he was able to keep the hotel going all the way until 1941 and the outbreak of WWII. Some of the very wealthy families who had built large mansions were also able to hold onto their wealth. While it is undoubtedly true that these residents most likely became thrifty in spending, they none-the-less, were able to afford items which helped to keep many local storefronts in business. Some of the shops on Lexington Avenue also made it through the crash and in fact Lexington Avenue would eventually rise up once more after the war. But overall, many families did suffer. Work became scarce, and it was hard to feed a growing number of children. The Magnolia of 1930 then became a mixture of what had been and what would be.

In Manchester and Beverly and Gloucester, the crash was also evident. Magnolia suffered more virtually due to size and resources while these other towns were able to invent new ideas to combat the downward trend. By no means however, should it be assumed that there were not shortages in every possible economic area. Today, our lives are much different then they were back then. While we are undoubtedly still "thrifty", that word had a much different connotation in 1929. Folks had to band together and help one another on a whole new level. Neighbors really went out of the way to help one another with even the simplest of tasks. Everyone knew that each person was suffering on some level and every individual pitched in. It was this helpful spirit that in some ways created an even deeper appreciation and understanding of what it was like to be a part of a community.

The communities of Manchester and Magnolia had grown and prospered. They had developed a rich tradition and seen a great immigration of people filled with many different cultures and histories. The jobs in the area had become diverse, the train had become a fixture of daily life, and goods and services had developed, as did tourism and hospitality. And now both towns were dealing with the national problem of a severe economic downward spiral and each dealt with it differently and with mixed results. However, in both cases, each place found comfort in the people who lived there and the communities became even stronger as a direct outcome of what was an unfortunate circumstance. As the 1920's came to a close the area looked much the same on the surface as it had previous to the market crash. When 1930 dawned, so too did a resolve to move forward and rebuild what had been lost. But it would not be easy on both a national as well as a local scale.

While this chapter has attempted to give a brief understanding on the history of these two towns it is by no means complete. The idea was to set the table as it were and give the reader a setting on how the towns formed prior to the Clifton Burke moving into Manchester. As the year 1930 continued to plod along and some of the governmental programs began to help stabilize the economy, the Burkes saw fit to begin to raise a family.

It would not be easy but then again they had the community to help and it was this community that Finney was born into.

CHAPTER THREE

Finney Arrives

It was during this period of time that John "Finney" Burke made his entrance onto the stage. On August 30th 1930, John Clifton Burke was born in Beverly Hospital. The Great Depression was in full swing and it was a time of great uncertainty. Manchester was suffering through the Great Depression as were most small New England towns and municipalities but as has been discussed the town continued to push forward. Jobs were undoubtedly scarce and most folks were in the habit of hoarding what little extra money they had for fear of things getting worse. The banks had become quite stringent with funds by this time and the public had seen its fair share of "bank runs". Most folks had even begun to put what little money was left into jars or under mattresses as opposed to trusting the American banking system. There is still a large population of Depression kids that keep money stashed away even today. In the end, the one thing that the Great Depression taught people was the importance of money, how not to waste it, and even more importantly what one should do to make sure it never ran out.

Through the roaring twenties people had learned to let go and spend more freely. Now John Clifton "Finney" Burke was being brought into a world that had grown quite different. His family had managed through the first year of the Depression and Finney was brought home from the hospital to a nice house down off the center of town. Healthy and happy Finney was about to enter into a family that had become quite well known and very much loved and respected in town.

Finney's father Clifton Lowell Burke was one of the lucky ones. He had a solid job working for the Boston and Maine railroad. While this did not afford the family much in luxury, it was at least a steady income during a trying time. He was born and raised in Rowley and his family was in the leather business. Finney's grandfather, John C. Burke, whom Finney is named after, had a warehouse in Ipswich that stored vast quantities of leather products. The leather industry on the North Shore was second only to the fishing industry. Everything from shoes to handbags was mass- produced for export, mainly to the European continent. The Burke's business was two fold. The family was in what was coined the first phase of leather production. The company prepared leather for the insoles of shoes. They also produced secondary items like handbags and leather for hats and jackets.

Overall the business was prosperous but Finney's dad Clifton had no desire to stay in the leather business. It was the railroad that enticed him from an early age. Whether it was by divine intervention or just pure luck, Clifton's move toward becoming a railroad man as opposed to a leatherback was a fortuitous one. Soon after the crash of 29' the leather business imploded. Of all the industrial businesses, the leather industry suffered the worst. Factories closed, thousands of people were out of work, and cities like Lowell and Lynn really took it on the chin. Thus began a long slow demise of a once booming industry. The leather companies never recovered. By the time the New Deal had been imposed and the country began to climb back out of the economic depression, the shoe business had deteriorated and soon after the first glimpses of globalization began to take shape. The few businesses that weathered the depression now sought cheaper ways to make the goods they produced. This opened up the possibility of producing goods in other countries, which only added to the further demise of places like Lynn and Lowell who had been built upon the great leather industry.

But Clifton sought out another way to make his means. The Iron Horses that rolled up and down the eastern seaboard caught his attention early on. The great Boston and Maine railroad, which carried the goods his family once plied, was the place Clifton set up shop soon becoming a freight service manager. The Boston and Maine was not only where Clifton found employment but also where he would eventually find a wife.

Finney's mother Anna Coughlin Burke, who was born and raised in Manchester, would also end up working for the railroad and, after marrying Clifton, Finney was brought up around the Iron Horses from an early age. During the early part of the 20th century most boys would follow in their fathers footsteps. If your father was a farmer then chances are you would most likely become a farmer too. Winding its way down the line from job to job, father to son, the economy continued to sputter along. The crash of 29' only accelerated the phenomena. Since jobs were more scarce sons looked to their fathers to help open doors in hope of gaining employment. Obviously the easiest route to employment was following right behind. Thus it could be assumed that John was no doubt going to become a train employee like Clifton.

Would this then be John Clifton "Finney" Burke's fate? From a job perspective it was not a bad way to go. The railway was the king of the land. New lines were being laid across the country daily. Even with the Depression in full swing, goods had to be delivered from North to South and East to West. Clifton was most likely in a position to help Finney gain entrance when the time came and most undoubtedly this was a proposed assumption amongst many in the family. College was always an option when Finney became of age, but it was hard enough to send a boy to college even in good economic times. Although one could not see how long the depression would last, it is most likely that college was not at the forefront in the minds of many parents in the 1930's. Finney was now settling into the town where his family was established.

The early 1930's were a time of excitement and hope mixed with turmoil and tragedy. Innovations continually developed to help increase production and goods continually became increasingly varied. The trains that Clifton worked on moved more and more merchandise and the train companies laid more and more tracks. Even though the country was suffering, the economic engine was still moving forward. The direct result for the Burkes was simple; Clifton was busy. From a very early age, Finney's father was not around as much as some fathers who worked in other industries. His office was in Boston and he would often need to work long days well into the evenings.

Because Finney's father was gone for long periods of time due to his job, his mother ran the household. The Burke house was raised Catholic. Finney's family attended the Sacred Heart Church and both were very active in the community. Anna sat on many of the church committees and was in charge of the annual Christmas party and the gathering of all the gifts and ice cream for the event. Clifton, Finney's father played the organ for the choir on Sundays and was also very much into music even outside of church. Finney could often remember his father playing music in the house.

The Catholic faith was strong in the Burke house and Anna ran the house as such. Reverend Lahey would make the rounds every two weeks and visit all of the houses in town that worshipped at his church and he could be found at the Burke household quite often. Finney's grandmother was also very religious and between Anna and Margaret, Finney got a good dose of Catholic virtue daily.

The Burke household was not an uncommon sight compared to other families in that one or more grandparents lived within the family unit. Many families during this period had multiple generations living with them. The family foundation filled with values and good moral upbringing that Finney received as a result cannot be calculated on paper. When meeting Finney, anyone can realize his worth within the first few seconds. Humility and a humble demeanor travel with Finney like a pair of old gloves. It is this trait above all others that Finney prides himself on.

In fact it was Finney's humbleness that gave rise to the difficulties surrounding trying to get his life down on paper. He has seen so much in his life and he is filled with stories that span decades; stories filled with many of the locals and most of the major events that took place over the past half century on the North Shore. However, he is so humble that he never wants any of the stories written for fear of upsetting someone. His poor wife has to remind him that most of the people he talks about have passed on. Such is life when you are eighty-five.

Even though Clifton was away much of the time, Finney always had an adult presence to help out when needed. Not to mention the fact that the family was intimately involved in the community. So Finney from early on was able to gain an incredible amount of protection and this allowed for a secure and fulfilling early childhood. His childhood would only blossom further as he entered his formative early educational years. Finney was bright and articulate as a boy and he was often seen milling about down at the local store listening to all the local gossip and chatter. This may have been a first wave of inner awareness that would end up resulting in his future love of telling stories.

As with most local towns the storefronts and parlors were where all of the action took place. Folks would come in daily to pick up the news and purchase goods. The newspaper was a central component to all that was happening. This is where everyone caught up not only on local happenings, but also allowed for inclusion in what was occurring nationally. Obviously due to the era, the national news was incredibly important. Unlike today, the newspapers were updated regularly throughout the day and delivered multiple times. This gave residents an opportunity to be aware of major events not too long after those events occurred. In todays world with the Internet and technology we have instant access to the news. Yet even then most residents were generally aware of what was happening on a global scale even if they were somewhat cutoff from where things were happening.

Many residents in Magnolia were also the "weekend" type. Finney would often go down to the train station and watch the Pullman cars come in on Friday afternoons. These cars were for the rich city tycoons who had built many of the large estates. They would come on the weekends and visit. This was another way for the local population to keep up on what was going on in the larger national stage.

Finney loved trains. Having a father in the train business helped fuel this passion. Finney loved to listen to his father's stories about the world of the railway and how trains traveled up and down the coast. Finney was a master at seeing organization and conformity. Understanding these ideas helped develop his skill as a newspaper reporter years later.

For the Burke family, the 1930's were coming to a close and Europe was embroiled in turmoil. Hitler had won the majority in Germany and had now taken over the entire country. The Nazi Party was on the move and Czechoslovakia had been invaded without any resistance. Most of Europe was in fear but no country came to aid the Czechs. America wanted to stay out of any European war having seen what WWI had done to the country as a whole. Out of 15 million inhabitants in Czechoslovakia, almost 4 million were German. It was an easy coupe for Hitler.

Back home in what could be only be described as a "million miles away", young Finney Burke was continuing to live a rather idyllic life. The Depression was over, the country was regaining its former economic engines, and most people wished for a prolonged peace and a chance to build some normalcy in their lives. Finney's parents went about their lives raising Finney and the rest of the family and life in Manchester and Magnolia moved forward.

CHAPTER FOUR

Finney Starts to "fit in"

Finney's grandfather, John C Burke had attended Dummer Academy as a young boy. He had gone on to build his leather business and in Finney's early years, John introduced Finney to one thing that would forever surround his life: baseball. John was a good player at Dummer. He played catcher. In those days this was the only position to wear a glove. The running joke was that John was smarter than the rest of the team and knew he would need his hands for working in later years so he volunteered to play catcher.

The love of baseball trickled down from John to Clifton and then to Finney. Thus, the household was a mixture of catholic reserve and baseball cheers. For Finney, baseball would become a lifelong passion. After Finney's grandmother on his fathers side passed away, Clifton went to

live with his uncle. Finney loved visiting his Uncle's place
because he knew there would be some form of baseball chatter
going on. Whether it was a game on the radio or just the
opportunity to talk about the sport, these trips were an
exciting time for a young boy. With Finney's father being away
so often it was also a good time for some good old fashioned
male bonding.

As stated earlier, both of Finney's parents were very
active in the community especially in church. Finney's mother
always helped out where she could but this was especially
evident when it came time for the yearly church social. Not
only was she put in charge of organizing the event, the special
treat of garnering ice cream was placed on her shoulders. This
was no small feat in the late 1930's. Forget the fact that it was
difficult to keep anything cold for very long in those days:
since not everyone owned a refrigerator and ice was not cheap.
Coming up with enough space to hold enough ice cream to
feed all the young children who looked forward to this day
each year was just as daunting a task. Then came the expenses
of purchasing all the ice cream. Today we take so much for
granted but in 1938 as Finney and his classmates waited for an
ice cream it was a big occasion. However, the family had a bit
of an "in" shall we say with a local ice cream producer by the
name of H. P. Hood. Anna was related to a man who worked
for the Hood Company and thus she was able to procure the

needed delicacy and get a good price to boot. This most assuredly held her in high esteem with the local families but it can be assumed that the local children regarded her most affectionately.

Manchester and Magnolia celebrated most summer holidays in the same fashion. The towns would swell with visitors even during the down times. Relatives would come to spend time by the seashore. And for Finney it was a time to be out of school and learn about the town he lived in. From early on he was an avid observer. This skill would serve him well in years to come as he embarked upon his career. While still young, Finney would often go into the center of town with his mother or grandmother to fetch goods from the local store and retrieve the daily post. He would also get to see the train as it rambled by. In the evenings he might even be allowed to meet his father as Clifton returned from the big city.

Finney's childhood was, in his eyes idyllic. Interviewing him and seeing that even now, 87 years on, his passion and love for the early years he spent in Manchester are still prevalent. And why wouldn't they be? His world was one filled with security, love, family, and a host of opportunities to learn about the greater society in which he lived. He was surrounded by information both locally and nationally. His father would return at night from Boston with all sorts of stories about the world outside of Manchester and during the day Finney would follow his mother and grandmother around and learn all he could about the local happenings. Finney's passion for his community is incredibly deep. Many of us have relatives that are those "diehard townies". The odd family member who eats sleeps and drinks with a love for what is close at hand and someone who wears the colors of the town with pride. Finney is one of these individuals times ten.

His mother also worked for the town library and in both unofficial and official positions in local government. She really was part of the lifeblood of the community. There was not much that occurred within the town's borders that she did not know about. Again, this tie to the community would come back to help Finney as he ascended the ranks in his job years later. His pride and thankfulness for his mother can also be seen.

His father was also a very admired person throughout the town and Finney was brought up to respect and value all people. This value system of treating all people the same would really come into play later on in his career. His Grandmother Margaret held firm the convictions set down in scripture and she made sure both Finney and his sister followed them as best they could. She was Roman Catholic and said the rosary at home daily. She would make sure that the entire family was all present and accounted for in church every Sunday. Dressing up in her finest, Margaret would stride down the lane towards church walking with a cane. Finney and almost everyone else knew she did not really need the cane but that it was used as part of the ensemble.

The whole notion of following the teachings of the bible and the commandments went even deeper for Finney. Part of his family of the previous generation had been raised in a black home and it was instilled upon Finney from an early age to treat all races with the same respect. The issue of race would follow Finney throughout his life. He is a man who does not see people by their skin but by their heart. It is those penetrating eyes, the eyes of a reporter that can see through color and get to the story. The ability for Finney to be able to see the story behind the story and break down the color barrier would also help him in later years. He is adamant when it comes to race equality. Many times in our lives we come across folks who preach for the betterment of others and equality for all. Finney believes this down to the core of his soul. Anytime our conversations would turn to a story regarding race, it would be the only time I could see a fire burn inside of Finney. He is an amazing man at always keeping his composure, but even at his age, when discussing race equality, the eyes would sparkle extra bright and his knuckles turn white.

Sometimes it is hard to see what truly means the most to a person. Many people can hide their emotions. Finney is like a chameleon. It is very hard to break down what he is feeling and get inside to what he is thinking. But when it comes to race, there is no middle ground. This stance would come to guide Finney years later as he dealt first hand with a major national crisis on a local level, which resulted in the Boston bussing incidents of the 1970's.

His grandfather John who was by this time living with Finney's uncle in Rowley had retired. His life still revolved around many things but most of all it revolved around baseball. John's love of baseball was unwavering. Finney continues to show the same passion. These are not your local average rainy day fans. A true baseball fan is a dying breed. The type of fan who has gone to Fenway for 60 years, sat in the same seat, eaten the same lunch a hot dog and a coke; these fans are the ones you hear about on the news after they have passed away. Any talk of baseball and those sparkling eyes light up. Well John was that type of fan.

He spent his life toiling away at his craft and providing for his family. People like John and Finney are in some ways the true hero's of a generation. We don't hear much about them, they aren't spilled all over the covers of magazines, and once they are gone many are often forgotten. Yet without these great people, the ones who are dedicated to what they do, our nation would not be what it is and our towns would not function. Baseball diehard fans are an analogy of these great people. They can sit through losing years and yet watch with that same hungry dedication. In Finney's future it was this one great trait, passed down from father to son, which may have been his greatest asset in his quest as a news writer. An unwavering dedication to the craft and to getting the story correct is what drove Finney every day.

These men work hard everyday and when they finally get a chance to rest they enjoy the simpler things in life like baseball. The other trait that makes these folks special is their reserve. People like Finney and his grandfather do not live their lives for glory or trophies. John, and now Finney live to serve others and enjoy those simpler things like baseball because that is what they were meant to do. So now with John in retirement, each day he would walk through town down to the local gas station. John would chat it up with the locals, read the newspaper and watch the world go by. Most of the people in town had a great respect for John and there is no doubt that everyone who lives a life like he did deserves that one special moment before he is gone. Many of us do not ever get to have that moment; but John did.

One afternoon, while John was taking up his customary stool in the garage, a car pulled up and the attendant went out to fill the tank. As the driver stepped out the attendant realized it was none other than Ted Williams, John's all time favorite ball player. The attendant, seeing an opportunity, told Ted about John and what an honor it would be if Mr. William's went in and quickly said hello. Now Ted was known as a pretty decent fellow but not altogether outgoing when he spoke with fans. However, he took the attendant up on his offer and went in to "chat" with John. What Ted thought would be a quick discussion lasted all afternoon. There they both sat discussing family, friends, and obviously baseball.

The times have changed of course. Today I am not sure if a life long baseball player in his waning years would get a chance to spend an afternoon with his idol. The story is a great analogy of what life was really like back then. Every generation has it's own struggles. The Depression was a challenge that Manchester and Magnolia faced and overcame as did countless other cities and towns across America. Yet, back then the attitudes and way in which people interacted on some levels were much simpler. John got his day. He was able to fulfill a lifelong dream of meeting Ted Williams and he received so much more than that. Finney was able to hear the story of Ted Williams and the gas station and carry that memory with him which only made his love for the game of baseball grow.

There were of course other skills that some of Finney's relatives enjoyed and when he was young he was able to benefit from these. The love of baseball he got from his Grandfather; but the love of food came from Margaret. You see Finney's Grandmother had quite a knack for cooking. In fact she was considered somewhat of a professional around town. Finney was subject to all kinds of "good eats" when Margaret got cooking her meals. She was so sought after that many times the hired help who ran the large estates would seek her out to come up to the house on days when large parties were to take place. She would move about, checking all the edibles to make sure they were cooked properly.

Margaret and her Irish friends would meet once a month to "gossip". It was sort of a ritual. The ladies would gather and the stories would flow. For Finney, this was a day to enjoy some very fine Irish pastries. Even today, that excitement still resonates with him. In doing this project, my wife and I have spent many wonderful afternoons in Finney's company along with his wife Irene. Of course each of these visits was never complete without pastries as I stated earlier. On these occasions, watching Finney "sneak" an extra pastry when Irene wasn't looking always made my wife and I chuckle and I thought back to those times long ago when Finney undoubtedly did the same thing with his grandmother. He may have aged considerably but the young boy spirit from the 1930's was still prevalent in an aging body eight decades later.

Summers for Finney during his early years were just as carefree as the random meeting had been between John and Ted. For most boys there were chores to do and of course church on Sunday but overall both towns, Manchester and Magnolia really encompassed what we today think of as the foregone relaxed summer seaside towns of the past. Yet growing up in Manchester, Finney and his friends and all the other full time residents were able to gain such a different perspective on the larger world than maybe other small communities in the area were able to enjoy due to the railway service and the summer residential boom. Finney also was different in that he did not partake in the normal chores that other children usually were subjected to. From a very young age Finney was employed in another type of labor as we shall see.

The town of Magnolia's population in 1930 only stood at 2,636. By no means a large town but compared to the census of 1890 when the town only had 1789 residents, there had been a considerable increase. Yet in the summer this population would double. While the summer residents were not officially counted on the census, the town during the summer took on a whole different atmosphere. Beginning in 1845 when Richard Dana built the first large-scale mansion along Manchester's coastline, people had flocked to the area. Manchester is not a very large area, encompassing just 18.3 square miles, but with such a small permanent residential population there was plenty of coastline to build on. Soon, news spread and by the turn of the 1880's a mini boom in construction was taking place. The greatest of these houses was constructed in 1883 and was named Kragsyde. It was built by George Nixon Black and unfortunately torn down in 1929 the year before Finney was born. The destruction of the house coincided with the Market crash.

However by the time Finney was seven and allowed to freely roam the center of town with an understanding of the greater world around him, most of the large mansions still remained. As the economy slowly rebounded so to did the steady stream of summer visitors. For Finney and the other children in town this must have been a great time. They were able to see and learn about people of wealth and watch the town swell with activity. Of course there was also the Oceanside Hotel that catered to a whole separate contingent of summer residents, those folks who came just for the sun and beach and to vacation at the hotel. The local economy obviously benefitted greatly.

The influx of summer migrants also meant that there were more children to play with. Finney's grade school class numbered in the teens so it was hard enough to find a full team to play ball let alone just to play other games. In the hazy days of summer there were plenty of new faces to interact with. And, even from a small age, the talk would usually center on baseball. Today it is hard for the younger generation to understand the depth that the game permeated in everyday life. Baseball truly was king. Robert Creamer writes in the PBS series on baseball dealing with the thoughts surrounding the game in the 1930's: "There wasn't a lot of money around in the depression years, and the lack of money gave the game a measure of intimacy, a kinship with the people that it hadn't had before and hasn't had since. More than ever, baseball reflected the times."

For Finney and the rest of the boys who called Manchester home in 1938 baseball was a way of bridging all gaps. The gap in socio-economic class, the gap that could be found between the permanent and summer residents, and even the gaps that may have occurred between different cultures with the increases in immigrants were all melted away when discussing the game of baseball. And no other team meant more to the inhabitants of Manchester and Magnolia than the Boston Red Sox. The Babe had come and gone, retiring in 1935 but the rivalry between the Sox and Yankees was hotter than ever. 1938 saw both teams open the season playing each other and going toe-to-toe, right up until the last series of the year when the Yankees took the pennant.

Finney was still very young in 1938, just a small child, but he knew about baseball even then. And the local boys had plenty to talk about in 1938. All the children had plenty of fun playing baseball and pretending to be Lefty Grove or Jimmy Foxx. The idyllic summer of 1938, Finney was eight years old and already a well-known young man about town. He was able to enjoy playing with the local boys and girls and also begin to learn about how the world worked. Again, that wonderful gift of observation began to formulate ideas in his head. He would watch the train roll into town each day and hear his father talk about what it was like to work on the railroads. He would watch the post delivered house by house. Finney was also drawn towards the way the newspapers were delivered. News it seems interested Finney very much. And it would also seem that he was growing up at a time when news both locally and nationally were about to take a massive turn towards the catastrophic.

The country had weathered a storm, the Great Depression. Roosevelt had passed through sweeping new ideas to stimulate the economy. National roads had been built up across the land. Bridges had been constructed to put people back to work. The National Park Service had become the largest employer in the country by way of the New Deal. And in Manchester, the town had overcome the odds and in some ways even flourished next to a present danger of economic ruin. Finney and the Burke household remained steady. Clifton's job was doing well, and Anna was as busy as ever in local town affairs. Finney was about to enter 3rd grade and all seemed well with the sole exception that the Yankees had bested the Red Sox that year.

However on September 21st 1938 the first major news story that Finney was old enough to be a part of and remember hit; The Hurricane of 1938. Sweeping up the east coast the hurricane slammed into New York City. This of course was prior to storms being named but the destruction from the Hurricane of 38' has never been repeated in the North East and not a person alive in 1938, had not been made aware of its impact. The Newspapers coming in from Boston to Magnolia and Manchester told of the horrific catastrophe. Whole houses were being swept away. There were many deaths including two people who tried to exit a stranded train and were blown away. In Westhampton alone, 29 people would lose their lives and 149 homes would be destroyed. Sitting back in Manchester and hearing these stories must have had a profound effect on young Finney. News it would seem was something he was very much interested in but it was not just the news stories that really peaked his curiosity; it was how the news was delivered. Even at eight years old Finney was bitten by the news bug.

1938 was now coming to a close. It had begun much like any other year yet it had finished with a hurricane and a sensational news story that few had been prepared for. However with the dawning of 1939, things in Manchester seemed to revert back to business as usual. Finney was now in 3rd grade, baseball and trains were still on his mind, but news was a medium that the young Finney was beginning to pay very close attention to. And in 1939 there would be plenty of it.

CHAPTER FIVE

Finney Comes of Age

Many speak of young children today as growing up too fast. With technology, the children today have access to many things that parents were once better able to control. Information is right at a child's fingertips and can be viewed in an instant. Technology has given us great advantages in how quickly we are able to get news and how quickly we can respond but this is not always a good thing. Yet it has led to the idea that somehow children are growing up faster than in previous generations. After interviewing Finney and creating this book, I would argue that children in the 1930's grew up at the same rate but just had different ways of maturing as shall be shown.

Finney had an aunt who lived in Beverly on Elliot Street near the railroad tracks. Now entering his 9th year,

Finney was allowed to go with his father on occasion to visit. At nine, Finney was very much in love with trains and baseball. News and the importance of keeping people aware of what was going on was also beginning to develop in his young mind. Sitting in his aunt's house and watching the trains ramble by going either North or South, Finney wondered what it would be like to follow in his parent's footsteps. His aunt was encouraging and loved to have Finney over to watch the trains. It seemed as if most of young Finney's life revolved around the Iron Horse. How then could he not become a railroad man himself?

The most interesting part of interviewing Finney and hearing about how his early life developed was in getting a sense that Finney is truly unique. While it is true that at nine most boys are not thinking about careers and such, Finney was so utterly aware of all the surrounded him it only made sense to wonder and ponder these larger questions. Of course he was also still a boy of nine, so playing professional baseball was always an option. In all seriousness, Finney was drawn to trains from a young age but now the idea of the dissemination of news affected him differently than other boys.

Trains were exciting and fun to play with and be around. He had even been given a model train set as a gift. This was no small gift back in those days. The only problem was that Finney knew everything there was to know about trains. He had grown up around them. However the model train he was given was wrong. It had three rails. A complete stickler for accuracy, Finney took the third rail out. Of course in a model train this is the rail that supplies the power to make the train move. Suffice as to say, Finney did not receive any more model train sets in the future. But the event brought to light another great attribute that Finney had, the gift of accuracy. Observation and accuracy are two of the most important elements when dealing with news. These two extremely important traits were to serve Finney very well in the future.

If Finney was not going to be a conductor or manager for a train company, then what would he become? A baseball player perhaps? John C. Burke A.K.A. Finney loved the game. It was in his blood and like most young boys there were moments, standing on the diamond and pretending to be some famous player when the thoughts would run through the mind...maybe, just maybe I could be a pro. But talking to Finney is like talking to a mirror that can only tell you the honest truth Finney just wasn't good enough. And, from a very young age he knew it. Yet how does a boy who loved the game as much as he did give up on that dream so quickly? In fact John "Finney" Burke is nicknamed after Lou Finney of the

Boston Red Sox. It is a nickname that he received as a young boy and a name that has stuck with him for eight decades.

Lou Finney was a first baseman for the Boston Red Sox in 1939 and played with them until 1945 with a brief two-year hiatus due to WWII. In one particular game Lou belted out three hits all triples. He was not a power guy but he was fast. Finney was also fast, really fast. On the same day that Lou Finney belted out those three triples, John Burke was playing baseball with some friends. He also repeated the same feat that Lou Finney accomplished on the exact same day. From that moment onward John Burke became "Finney". This story again shows just how much baseball meant to Finney. But it wasn't just Finney. Baseball really was the national pastime. Most newspapers followed the game almost religiously. The stories and bylines of the game were not relegated to some back page. Boys throughout America grew up with baseball as a major connection between themselves and their fathers. Today, we have so many other sports that people are interested in. When Finney was growing up there were other sports as well. But in the minds of most, there was only baseball.

Talking to Finney years later though and it is obvious that baseball was not going to be part of his career choices. He will tell you himself that he was just an average player. The twinkle in his eye though tells you that he knows he had at least one skill above most other players. If he could just get on base then he was lights out fast. "Get me on first and I'll always find second". That was Finney's game. He never hit for power but always tried to get on base. The way he tells about his skill and the honesty with which he discusses his baseball prowess only add to the already perfectly aligned traits Finney displayed from a young age that would help him immensely in his future career.

There is a complete modesty to him. He is humble but it goes beyond that. When talking sports especially amongst men, modesty can sometimes go out the window and be replaced with fish stories. Never once has a boy not embellished upon his sporting skill; the proverbial "one that got away", or "I almost had a hole in one". With Finney you receive a sense of downplaying his skill and sporting prowess. Which, as a writer and listening to him makes me wonder if there is not more to his actual sports abilities than he lets on. A man who does not embellish on his sporting ability is a man worth trusting. Finney is one of these people.

Between 1940 and 1941 much occurred which would forever change the lives of many. None around the world would be isolated enough to not feel the effects of WWII. In Manchester and Magnolia, the newspapers continued to tell the story of what was happening in Europe. Up until this

point, Finney now nearing the age of eleven had been aware of
what was happening but, like most kids, he was insulated
somewhat directly. The United States had for the most part
been kept out of the war. The government had been sending
supplies to European friends, but talk of entering a full scale
global war was continually disregarded. Most people were
weary from having to fight through the depression. And many
more still remembered the onslaught and total waste of life
that had resulted from WWI. The topic was often a heated one
and on a local level it split families and communities apart.
The ties and bonds were strong for many communities
between America and Britain and even France. But the nation
had suffered so much and had finally begun to pull itself
together and move forward. The economy was gaining
strength, communities were healing after losing so many young
lives in WWI, and most people really did not want to see a
return to all out war.

Yet all this changed on December 7th 1941 with the
attacks on Pearl Harbor. Instantly and overnight America
changed. While it is easy to see how this change would affect
the nation on a large scale, for Finney and the Burke family the
changes were a reflection of what would take place to families
across the country individually. Finney's father, being in the
railroad business would now be shipping much different cargo
up and down the east coast. President Roosevelt's now

infamous speech "Yesterday December 7th, 1941, A day that will live in infamy", was played on every radio in America. The United States could not stand by any longer and watch their allies suffer.

The War was to change the face of the earth. For Finney, it would also harken in a new understanding of what was going on around him on a much larger scale. All small towns throughout America would be utterly changed. The divisions that separated individuals were now gone. America woke up on December 8th united. What the Japanese failed to do was annihilate the American fleet at Pearl Harbor. And this was their ultimate mistake. As was heard by Admiral Yamamoto, Japan had awakened the sleeping giant.

America, while not prepared for all out war, was united. On a local level, most people knew that the war would change their daily lives on a profound way. For the Burke's, this was definitely the case. Finney was now eleven and well aware of most events that were taking place. His "tween" years would be affected by many issues that inevitably helped to mold his senses and push him towards the idea of the importance of disseminating information. The news was beginning to leave a lasting impression on young Finney Burke. And WWII was the backdrop for this newly deepened appreciation of the importance of newsprint.

There were so many outside forces that helped push Finney in the singular direction of becoming a journalist. Some of these reasons were on a larger scale and some very intimate. On the macro level, the news of the 1940's was of course sensational. Yes, for many in the town of Manchester, 1942 began much the same as any other year locally with the exception that a draft had been implemented and food rationing had begun. The trains were hustling by with additional cargo as the Nation prepared for war.

Finney still went to school each day and attended church on Sundays. The only difference was that he was now old enough to be an alter boy. As with much of this book, there are stories that Finney felt uncomfortable about putting into print. His humility and care for other people have developed into a very cautious approach as to what should be written. However Irene has given her blessing and I shall side with her. When you live for eight decades, most of the people who are part of these stories are no longer with us. This is the case when Finney discusses playing cards in church. The Alter boys used to sneak in decks of cards and play during Sunday mass. One day, unfortunately for Finney, he got caught. His Grandmother was none to happy. Watching Finney tell this story was quite interesting. You could see the anguish and still to this day the disappointment Finney felt in being caught.

However, this one story is the perfect analogy on Finney's character. The story by today's standards is pretty light fare comparative to many of the things children attempt to get away with. Most of us have done far worse things than play cards during sermon. Yet, Finney's character shows through. Imagine someone 70 years later being distraught over a card game and worrying about upsetting someone by telling the story? This is why John C. "Finney" Burke was made to tell the news. It is his character and morality that allow for telling the tales of other people in an honest way.

The war years also brought about new opportunities for Finney to hone his newly found craft. The news bug had hit him squarely. It all began with the local mailman who happened to have the same first name as Finney. John was also a news buff. Each day he would deliver the mail and if he saw anyone he would pull out a small notebook that he carried in his back pocket and ask for news tips. This entire process fascinated Finney.

Now, in the 1940's there was plenty of news to go around. Finney too, was expanding his realm of contacts in much the same way as John with his mail delivery. Finney had gotten a job delivering newspapers.

At the same time, many of the boys Finney's age were being asked to take on new roles in the town. Most of the adult men had gone off to war. A Civil Defense league had been created and Finney's father was in charge of the Manchester branch. Watch Towers had been constructed along the coastline to keep an eye on the water for incoming enemy boats. Most of these were German U-boats. Since there were few adult men to man the towers, most of the teenage boys were employed to do this. Although the reasons behind why the towers were there was sad, the time spent manning them for a young boy was quite exciting. Being able to stay out late into the night and look for enemy movements was something that gave Finney even more independence and a continued increased desire to understand all that was happening around him. Finney was also allowed to take specific classes taught by the Civil Defense on how to spot enemy planes. Another reason why the younger boys were employed in jobs they would never have had the chance to do previously, was quite simply, their eye sight was better.

The war continued to change how daily life was lived. Many families opened their homes to soldiers who were moving through the area on their way to some far off land. Strangers took up residence for a night and were served a warm meal. Finney remembers this time with a keen excitement. The Civil Defense office was upstairs in the firehouse that naturally meant that Finney now had access to the firemen as well. His entire life became surrounded by stories.

Crocker's boat yard in Manchester was building sub-chaser boats. Finney and the rest of the older boys in town were actually allowed to leave school early anytime there was a launching and cheer on the new boat as it put out to sea. Other opportunities for work arose due to the lack of manpower in town. Of course, the winters also brought snow, which meant an increase in snow shoveling business, but the boys were also involved in helping to spot and put out fires.

The church remained a bastion and central spot for the Burkes and others to gather in town. Everyone helped out with efforts for the war and with whatever each of them needed. Throughout 1943 and 1944, the town continued to stand firm, the watchtowers were manned, and everyone did their part.

Then in mid 1944, late one night, Clifton came into Finney's room and told him to get dressed. Clifton was still employed by the train company and his job had been very difficult. Much of the cargo remained the same. During this period many supplies were transported by train up and down the coast by the B and M railroad and Finney's father was in charge of making sure those goods got where they needed to go.

However, there were now other types of cargo that were being shipped. Troops were taken in the trains, always with window shades drawn down, to various ports. Unfortunately caskets of returning dead were also part of the war cargo. On this particular night however, the trains were vastly larger. The engines were straining under the weight of all the extra pull cars. Finney rode with his dad alongside these trains as they wound there way up the coast towards an ocean port. The shades remained down and, although Finney did not understand exactly what was happening, the feeling was intense. Finally, at one point, his father stopped. Finney saw before him train after train and out of these trains poured troops. Many troops. They boarded sea transports that were waiting to take them out to massive ships in the distance. Finney was in awe over the vastness of the entire operation. His father told him to never speak of what he saw that night.

The next morning, a Saturday, a deafening roar could be heard. The entire Burke household shook as if there was an earthquake. Looking up Finney saw wave after wave of P-48's and B-52 bombers overhead. So many it blackened the sky. The following week was June 7th D-day.

The entire experience of watching this massive operation unfold from a local perspective gave Finney newfound resolve that news was an incredible tool that could be used to understand the world. But he was still young. He had witnessed much already. And he had secured his first ever "real" job delivering newspapers. He had begun with only four customers but within a year he was delivering news to forty. One of the places he got to deliver to was the Essex Country Club. Here he got to meet many famous faces at a very young age. Yes, Finney had been bitten by the newspaper industry and by news in general. He was not yet 14 but the seed had been planted and with a little care it was about to grow.

CHAPTER SIX

The Newspaper Years

Finney was industrious. He liked to work. He had garnered a paper route and was expanding his clients. He worked for the Filias family who owned a shoe shine store as well. Finney always said he was a hard working shoeshine boy but he could never get the towels to snap the right way. Watching him talk about his youth and working at the Filias store, one could get a sense of just how important that time period was to him.

The most exciting working times for Mr. Filias came on the weekends when all of the wealthy families came from the city. On Saturday nights there would undoubtedly be dances at the Oceanside Hotel. As such, the men would need their white shoes shined for the event. The shoes would be polished and Finney would run them up and down off of the roof of the Filias store where the shoes were left to dry in the sun after being polished. Rainstorms of course were always a threat during this time. So Finney, being quick on his feet was asked to stay and watch over the shoes if the threat of inclement weather was about.

At the same time, Finney had begun to expand his newspaper delivery service. He had started out with only four customers but soon, he was delivering to 40. The Newspapers back then would be delivered multiple times per day. Finney would get the AM paper and deliver it to his customers prior to school. Then in the afternoon he would deliver the New York Times. This was followed immediately in the evening with another delivery of the Boston Traveler and the Globe and the American. On Sundays the papers were much heavier. Mr. Filias had an old car and replaced the running boards along the edge with larger boards that could support the newspapers and he would ride around and help the boys deliver the news.

As a 13 year-old boy this was quite an amazing and complex job. Thinking of the children today, I would harken to say that this type of work even outside of school hours just would not be possible. The laws alone would preclude most kids from partaking in such a job. Yet, back then young Mr. Finney was a budding entrepreneur. Of course Finney's favorite place to deliver the newspapers was the Essex Country Club. It was here that he really began to get excited about not just delivering news, but reporting on it. So much went on at that club. The business leaders discussing the events of the world, the sports stars coming in for tennis matches, and the local discussions over general topics, all made Finney want to learn about the delivery of news more.

In Manchester there was a family by the name of Singleton. John Singleton ran a local taxi service. Helen, his wife was the local correspondent for the Beverly Times. By the time Finney was 14 he was well known around town already as someone who loved the news. He was also regarded as a hard working boy. Helen, due to issues surrounding the post-war had to give up her job with the Beverly Times. Finney's name immediately came up as a replacement. Thus officially began Finney's career in journalism and the world of news.

He began as a sports writer. This is a job Finney loved. He saw an opening though to expand on this realm of reporting and convinced the Times to also report on local bowling scores. Since Finney was paid by line for his work it was a direct way for him to earn more money. At the same time, Finney was also in charge of the high school newspaper that he had started. So by the time he was knee deep in high school, Young Mr. Burke was already head long into the newspaper industry. Like the Times, Finney reported mostly sports events with the high school newspaper. He also dabbled in reporting on school functions like dances and such. The school newspaper gave Finney a platform to try different types of news reporting which also helped when it came time to ascend the ranks at the Times.

However, even during all of this, Finney was also reporting for the Manchester Cricket. After listening to Finney discus his early break into the news industry I asked Finney about his schoolwork. I could not believe one person could do all of this and also go to school. In the end, I found out that Finney did indeed finish his high school career and even managed to do all right with his grades. He was never a great student but he was definitely a good juggler and a proven reporter by the time he graduated.

News reporting was not his only job. He also quickly became known as a polished photographer. Finney saw a definite advantage to this. He could arrive on the scene of a story, report upon what was happening and then take photos thus creating a second job within the scope of a singular one. His tenacity and thriftiness served him well. The local police chief saw this as an advantage right away. And by the time Finney was a senior, he had his own police radio in his room.

Having a radio allowed Finney to hear about stories as they were breaking. It opened up an entire new way to report. Finney was soon depended on by the police so much that when larger stories broke he was even taken from school and went with the police chief to the scene of the story. He quickly became the main correspondent for the town of Manchester but even this job did not last long as he continued to move quickly through the ranks. Eventually his mother took over in his place as the correspondent while Finney continued taking on new roles and jobs. Finney graduated from Manchester High School in 1948 with a class of 17 students. It was now time for him to take his career to a new level.

Finney had grown up in a time of great social and economic change in the country. He was born during the Depression, had witnessed WWII, and seen the immense growth after the troops had returned home. He was industrious and had a knack for producing quality work at a young age. Blessed with a complete understanding of work ethics and a desire to want to convey the truth to society, Finney truly was born to write the news.

Between 1947-1949 Finney held many positions. He was the correspondent for Manchester to the Beverly Times, he wrote the sports column and even worked at the Herald as a correspondent as well. Working from 6AM-2PM at the Times, he would then turn right around and work for the Herald from 2-Midnight. It was a grueling schedule but one he was born for. Finney had the stamina, work ethic, and desire to succeed in the news industry.

Throughout it all, Finney was led by a great group of mentors. Even today, the people who helped Finney ascend the working sphere are held in high esteem as he reflects back on his years in the news. He never forgets where he came from or who helped him get there. His coach Joe Hyland, who went on to have paralysis in his later years, always pushed Finney to take the right direction. People like Mr. Filias were there to support him at a young age. Philip Weld, the owner of the Gloucester Times, upon seeing Finney's potential, urged him to find employment in a larger city newspaper so as to broaden his horizons.

Even the police chief helped with Finney's career. Being both reporter and photographer had its perks. However, it wasn't always easy. Many times Finney would have to photograph a crime scene and even be asked to take autopsy photos. This was a very hard thing to do. These were people who were friends or neighbors.

Finney remembers back to his first major accounting of a murder scene. A couple had been murdered and left in the woods. Finney had to photograph everything. As I interviewed him you could still pain in remembering the scene. Eventually though, the killer was found. On lighter assignments Finney was able to photograph the tennis stars that called Essex Country Club home in the summer. This is where he befriended Maureen Connelly. At the time she was the greatest tennis star of her generation. In fact, Finney escorted her to a baseball game and for him this is still an amazing point in his life.

As Finney's career began to escalate, so did the stories he was able to cover. He was so quick at ascending the ranks that it rankled some in the newspapers he was employed at. However, this ascent was quite simply that Finney was not just good at his job; he was great. Born into this career once Finney was given the true opportunity he flew like a hawk.

Weather always played an exciting role in his job as well. And it undoubtedly mixed with his family. On one day Finney was called out to a train wreck on the Swampscott line. It had been snowing heavily and Finney was nervous because he thought his father might be on the train. His thoughts raced back to his youth and the days he would spend with his dad at work. "I got to sit at his big desk and on Saturdays it was an extra special day. We could order a chicken sandwich and a Coke". In the end, his father was not on the train that day but talking about it reminded Finney about his one other favorite item: Coke. Finney loves Coca-Cola. His favorite line is, "fortunately every place I ever worked had a Coke machine. If it hadn't, I'm not sure how the news would have gotten reported."

By 1957, Finney had really settled into his career at the Beverly Times. In May all hell broke loose! It was from this point on that a series of sensational stories broke over the next twenty years that would shape Finney's career.

On May 8th 1957, a smoldering fire began in a section of woods outside the town line of Manchester. The weather for May had been rather dry and a pretty steady wind had begun to blow. What happened over the next few hours was a perfect combination of climate conditions that took the small smoldering fire and whipped it up into an inferno of massive proportions the like of which the North Shore had never seen. Within a day, the fire had consumed 10 acres and was threatening the entire town. Chief Hammond shouted again and again over a two-way radio for help and more help. Towns from as far away as New Hampshire came in to help. But in the end it looked hopeless. Finney was called in to report on the entire battle as it raged. For three days he barely ate or slept.

The inferno was only growing in size. Chief John Calley of Beverly was battling the west side and Hammond the right. The decision was made to send in a group to try and cut the blaze in half. Finney continued to report on the event and watched as these brave men went headlong into the fire in an attempt to cut the fire in two. Captain Donald Burgess led this heroic charge but before long the group became surrounded. For Finney, this news reporting was when he was at his best. Stating the facts was what was most important. People counted on the news. They counted on Finney to get the job done right. And report he did.

Somehow the brave men who attempted to cut the blaze were pulled out in time but the fire only continued to grow. Even townspeople stepped in to help. One large mansion, the first major home in the direct line of the fire was continually poured upon by water from a bucket brigade. Somehow by a miracle the home was saved. Many times over and over countless acts of heroism ensued and Finney was there to report upon them. Yet, however hard the men and woman fought, the blaze it just kept coming. A strong westerly wind was the culprit. And even with all of their training the fire departments in the area were just not used to battling this type of blaze.

However, just when all hope was fading something odd occurred; the winds just died. One firefighter was quoted as saying, "it was like a switch had been turned off". Finney, exhausted, smelling like soot, and hungry, returned home. The next day was a joyous one in which he was able to report that the town had been saved.

But sensational fires were not over with yet for Finney. As 1958 dawned another major event was about to unfold. Finney by now was well known and respected as a journalist. He was working as a major player at the Beverly Times and still had his photography as well. Using his two- way radio and contacts he always seemed to be in the right place at the right time.

One fateful night Finney received a call that the famed Oceanside Hotel in Magnolia was on fire. The roads into Magnolia had been cut off. Finney was able to get in with the help of his connections to the police department. Stealing off and driving through thickets and right across the Essex Club golf course he was able to get to the hotel and report first hand on the account. It was a sad state to report upon. The entire hotel was ablaze. The fire departments were now trying desperately to keep the flames from spreading. For the second time in a year, Finney was in the midst of the most sensational story in the area. And he did his job to perfection.

The hotel had been through so much. It had survived the Depression, made it through WWII, but now it was utterly destroyed. Finney reported on the aftermath. The hotel was gone but the town had been spared and yet again, stories of heroism ensued. But Magnolia would never be the same. Lexington Avenue and the local businesses had suffered for years. The one constant draw had been the hotel. Without this, Magnolia would be hard pressed to continue with viable local businesses. And it was true.

Other major news events followed. Finney in fact almost got killed one night when a fugitive escaped and stole a car in Newburyport. The man was armed and dangerous. A chase ensued and ended up in North Beverly where the fugitive escaped into the local woods. Finney was brought on scene to report. Being the hands on reporter that Finney was he of course went out into the woods to follow the hunt. The Police became separated from Finney and before long he was alone. He did not know it but the fugitive happened to be hiding in the same field that Finney was standing in. In the end, the Police were able to surround the field, extricate Finney, and all ended well. But reporting is dangerous work especially when you put all you have into getting to the heart of the story.

Even when not reporting in the field, Finney often found himself the center of news. The Beverly Times was produced on Cabot Street directly across from a large multi story building. One afternoon Finney was sitting at his desk when a call came across his radio that a large fire had started on Cabot Street. It was in fact the building directly across for the Times. The entire building was engulfed. Hoses were run from the hydrants on both sides of the roadway. The problem was that the road pitched downhill back towards the Times building. In the end, all the water from the hoses ran back down the street and right into the basement of the Times. The basement was where the printers were kept. Finney was now reporting on the fire and the fact that the Times building was being flooded and he was not sure if the printers would be ruined. It was a perfect trifecta of reporting the news. There never seemed to be a dull moment.

Finney spent many years reporting and editing for the Beverly Times. At the same time he was continually pushed by outside forces to grow his craft and seek a larger audience. In 1964 Finney left the Beverly Times and headed to the Haverhill Journal. He quickly became editor and had a much larger audience. But his roots remained in Manchester. He would travel to work but continued to live in Manchester. However, the news industry keeps odd hours. One never knows when a story might break. When late nights were warranted, Finney could stay with his sister who lived near where he worked in Haverhill.

He had already seen and reported on so much over the decade plus in the news business. On a local level, sports, weather events, sensational fires, and even the occasional murder kept him very busy. But as stories developed nationally on an ever more sensational level and as Finney moved from small town paper to mid level city paper, the national news took on an increased role in his reporting.

It was while he was working at the Haverhill Journal that Finney had to report on his first larger than life national news story; the assassination of President Kennedy. Finney's strong beliefs on human rights and equal rights when it came to minorities played a strong role in the difficulty he had in reporting on Kennedy's death. In interviewing Finney I could still see the anguish he felt over the assassination even after all the years had passed. It was easy to see that Finney placed Kennedy in a special place as someone who fought for all the right principles. In fact it was very hard to get Finney to discuss this story. But even harder was the major story that embroiled Finney years later as shall be shown.

In 1965 Finney was let go by the Haverhill Journal. Mr. Loeb who owned the paper was unhappy. Finney is firmly convinced that he felt threatened by Finney's liberal stance on issues and reporting. Finney believed in rights of others and the Journal was, in short, incredibly conservative. What might have been a down time for Finney's career actually became a wonderful opportunity. He finally had the chance and the pedigree to go after a job at one of the large city newspapers. His first stop was the Boston Herald. This job did not last long and ended rather quickly but it did however open the door to his final ascent: the Boston Globe.

Hired as a copy editor on the night desk in 1965, Finney had made it all the way from delivering newspapers for Mr. Filias to working at the Boston Globe. In 1966 he made assistant night editor and this quick promotion really caused a stir in the Globe. But again, Finney was very good at his craft. He covered many local news stories during this time period and many of these involved large fires. In Swampscott there was quite a large blaze that destroyed the New Ocean House and the Gloucester Hawthorne also went up in flames. But on the national scene things were beginning to heat up in Vietnam and the entire issue surrounding civil rights was ongoing.

Both of these incidents came to a head in 1974. Finney had to report on the fleeing of troops from Saigon and the utter loss of the war in Vietnam while at the same time dealing with the Civil Rights incident and the Boston bussing crisis. These were some of the toughest years of Finney's life. While he had a challenging time with the entire Vietnam saga, it was the bussing incidents in Boston that affected him the greatest. The entire story and resulting actions were fueled with emotion. By now, Finney had met and been married to Irene. They had moved to Magnolia and lived in the house of their dreams. Finney would commute into work and these were long dark days. He had to edit and make decisions on a topic that ripped him apart internally.

The bussing crisis for Finney finally hit a climax on one fateful afternoon. The Globe, known as a liberal paper was reporting the story much as Finney would have, with facts and a leaning towards the rights of all. This did not sit well with many. Before long a mob had massed outside the Globe and the police were called in. Things continued to spiral downwards. The head of a movement basically against blacks, Pixey Palladino, fought against the Globe and Finney as editor calling it a "nigger loving paper". As the day wore on the mob grew. At the same time it was raining as hard as ever. Police on horses were brought in to keep the peace. As Finney put it, "there was wet horse shit everywhere". He was surprised anyone could stand being in the mob but it kept getting larger and the situation was getting close to exploding. The mob was now able to block the trucks from leaving to deliver the papers and the police were actually outnumbered.

Bill Taylor, the owner of the paper was there. He called Finney into his office and pleaded with him to go out and talk to the mob. Finney was in quite a situation. As day wore into night he decided to act. Stepping out into the darkness and the rain and the horse manure, Finney pleaded with the mob to back down. Somehow in the end he was successful. The trucks were able to get out and the news was delivered.

The entire incident has affected Finney for his whole life. Even now, discussing the bussing incident, I can see the pain in his face. His eyes sparkle with a smoldering light. It was such a challenging time. But Finney moved forward.

In 1978 his career was bustling. It was during this time that he and Irene decided to open a restaurant in Magnolia called The Patio. And what a time it was. The Patio opened on February 1st 1978. One week later the blizzard of 78 hit! The town was brought to a standstill. Roads were closed, food was scarce, and people were stranded. Finney could get around because he had his reporter badge and he continued to report upon the news. But Irene decided to do a wonderful thing. She opened The Patio to everyone. Since most had lost power the food was going to go bad anyways. Thus, the town was brought together and a sort of blizzard party at the restaurant was created. This was the start of a long lasting relationship of good cheer and friendship with so many local people. The Patio would go on serving the town for many years to come and Irene and Finney were blessed many times over for their caring spirit.

As the 1980's commenced many other news stories unfolded and Finney was right there to report upon them. The Space Shuttle Challenger explosion was another story that affected Finney greatly. As were the many elections that he covered.

At the same time Finney also helped to perfect the craft of how newspapers were put together. He was a journalist, a photographer, and editor, and now helped create a system called the twill. This system helped perfect the way newsprint was displayed on the actual paper. It helped to streamline the entire process and is still in use today. One thing that was very important to Finney is the idea that every great news writer needs to be a great newsperson. In short, they must know all facets of the job. Only then can a journalist truly understand the craft as a whole entity and reach their potential.

Throughout the remainder of the decade Finney continued to take on new roles within the Globe. He eventually became editor over larger regions and would travel quite a lot throughout New England. But his heart and his home always remained in Manchester and Magnolia. He would make sure to always give a helping hand to new recruits and made sure to take time to continually give back locally. Irene and Finney throughout the 1990's continued to develop friendships in the community, work at making The Patio a success and Finney continued to develop his craft. He was never one to sit back on his laurels and always continued to make sure he was front and center in reporting the news.

Now full on five decades had passed as a Newspaperman. Finney was well known, well respected, and had dedicated so much to learning his craft. The 1990's ushered in a new form of news medium with technology. And Finney was right there to meet it head on.

Finney was also deeply involved in another aspect of the Boston Globe. He was a main driving force behind the Globe's Secret Santa operations. Finney was always so passionate when it came to children. The Secret Santa gave him the direct opportunity to give back to children all across the commonwealth. The Globe Santa would continue to be a part of Finney's life well after his official retirement.

CHAPTER SEVEN

The Later Years

Finney retired from the Boston Globe on June 7th 1996. However, as was the case with Finney, he never really retired. He remained as a consultant for the next 14 years. While reminiscing about his years in the news Finney stated, "I feel my whole life is about journalism".

The Globe gave Finney quite a retirement party. It was an incredible evening filled with many grateful attendees. But Finney never wavered on his humility. He is so unbelievably thankful for all of the help he has received over the years. His family played such a large role in his life. The connections that he had when he started out due to the close- knit ties between the Burkes and the community helped Finney immensely.

But Finney also felt that his "extended" family in the newspaper business was also instrumental in helping him achieve all of his own dreams. Which, at the end of the day were really quite simple. Finney wanted to help. He wanted to help those less fortunate get started in the industry. He wanted to help where he could with gender and race inequality. He wanted to provide for his family. Yet above all, Finney wanted to make sure everyone got the news; proper news that was filled with honesty and truthful facts. Finney was adamant about this.

The retirement party was filled with people who not only cared about Finney the man, but also respected the type of service that he had given. Finney truly is a real newsperson. Finney received a plaque at his retirement party and he was able to reconnect with so many individuals. However, he was by no means done in the news industry. Even now, at his advancing age, there is no doubt that Finney could probably outdo most other reporters. That twinkle is still in his eye.

So Finney remained with the Globe in a consultant capacity working on the online news division. His greatest moments of elation came in helping young journalists find their way in the business. His one big request when working with the kids was that they never call him boss. Finney's ideals and humility never wavered regardless of how many titles he earned or what role he played in a job. His love of the news only increased over time.

The newspaper industry had indeed changed. Technology was implemented and online news was becoming more and more prevalent. Finney adapted to all of the change with relative ease. The main reason behind the smooth transition for him was the fact the basic news reporting principles remained. Any young journalist working under Finney realized this right away. Accuracy in all its forms must be adhered to. Each story, whether in standard print or online was doubly checked. Sources were scrutinized and Finney made sure that embellishments were left at the counter. The news was about facts. Good writing and factual news took care of itself and people were more appreciative of a well written factual story than one made up of fluff.

The "kids" who worked under Finney were also taught to respect each position in the overall scheme of the newspaper. He respected them and they respected him. But in order for a news story to be of quality, each person had a role to fulfill. This was also another great area of knowledge that Finney was able to teach in his waning years as a consultant. He had seen it all. He had been through all of the changes in newspaper production and even helped construct some of those changes. Finney was instrumental in his development of the "twill" system. This system is still in use today. It was Finney in part who helped devise a system of how many words would fit into a certain size column. The Twill system helped create a better, more efficient way of producing the paper. Finney was also there throughout the formation of technological advances in production. And, of course he had held just about every position a person can hold in the newspaper industry.

Most of the new journalists were incredibly lucky to have Finney take them under his wing. Some went on to work at some of the larger news stations and newspapers. The new recruits would gather the news and Finney would make sure no one jumped too soon with a story. This was one inherent problem embedded within technology. It was so quick. One could gather the news, type out the story and upload it in a tenth of the time as old print. But this came at a cost in the way of accuracy. Finney taught patience. He was the driving force behind making sure these kids did not over reach and end up producing something inaccurate.

However, as Finney puts it, "Technology dulled things". Especially when it came to elections. Television took the edge off of the importance of newsprint when it came to elections. In the past, folks would have to wait longer for results. This would allow for drama, discussion, heated debates, and an overall excitement. Now, television and technology allowed for the news to declare winners sometimes before polling stations were even closed!

But Finney was still involved in election coverage at the Globe all the way up until 2014. Finney has a fondness for covering elections, maybe second only to sports.

He also continued to oversee the Globe Santa stories. He would receive the stories and edit them. Not all stories were good ones. But news is news. There was one particular moment where Finney had to cover not a feel good Globe Santa story, but one of shame. One story involved a woman who lied about her situation so well that she actually was able to swindle gifts out of the Globe Santa fund. However, she was caught and Finney was there to report on it.

In 2005, all of Finney's dedication to his craft and to helping others was fully honored when he received the American Quill Award. This award was created to honor people in the industry who inspired reading and literacy. All fields of literature were included. Finney Burke was honored alongside J.K. Rowling, David McCullough, and Deepak Chopra to name a few. When pulling out the award to show me, I could tell how proud Finney is. Yet, that same humility is always present. Few folks in town realize that their very own Finney Burke received honors alongside some of these other household names.

Yet Finney, for all of his pride in winning this award, downplays it as "I was just doing my job". I wonder if he realizes how big of an honor that award is? I suspect he does, but it would not change how he acts. He is quite unique.

At the same time Finney was working hard everyday even though he was "retired", the family business "The Patio" continued to serve the people of Magnolia and all others who came for great food and good stories. Irene continued to work at the restaurant and Finney actually helped manage the bookkeeping. They both traveled a little to see family now that they had at least a little spare time. California was a destination but it was Portugal that held them dearly. Irene is Portuguese and many of her family members still live there. Finney and Irene traveled there and spent time. The stories they tell of the food, and culture and people make me very much want to take a holiday.

Finney also spent time putting some of his life's work together. He has a nice office in the house. Around the walls are scattered many pictures and awards. Of course, as we all have, there are always house repairs to keep Finney busy as well. The house that they live in is incredibly special to both of them. Finney loved the house and in fact dreamed of owning it well before they ever purchased it. The house is exactly as Finney and Irene would have it: warm and inviting. It is one of those homes where as soon as you step across the threshold you feel comfort. The sense is like you are already part of the family. Maybe it's the house, maybe its Finney and Irene, or maybe it is a combination of both; but whatever the case, the Burke home just feels good.

In 2010 Finney had just celebrated his 80th birthday. The Cape Ann Beacon Newspaper decided to reach out to Finney and ask him about his 80 years living in the area. Finney's answer, when asked about living in the same place for 80 years, was vintage Finney, "I love it here"! He really did not need to ever be anywhere else. There was enough happening on the North Shore of Massachusetts to keep Finney busy for an entire career and well into retirement.

In 2013 Finney and Irene decided to close the restaurant. This must have been an incredibly difficult decision. They had weathered so much and created such lasting customers. They had even gone through the recession in 2008 and remained steadfast. While other businesses along Lexington Ave closed, The Patio continued to be a beacon of unwavering commitment to the community. Yet, the time had come. They found someone to purchase the business and knew it was time to say goodbye to what had really become a local institution.

Over the past two years they have settled into a routine that still involves them in many ways with the community. Of course, Irene's famous Christmas party still brings together many people from the community each holiday season. And their love of good food has by no means dwindled. They still go out to dinner and socialize with neighbors and friends. Finney is still connected to the Globe and of course baseball still rules.

The house continues to add projects onto the list of things to do. The winter of 2015 affected the Burkes as it did most of us who live in the North East. Many repairs were needed on the house, and it was very tough for Finney and Irene to make it out much during those treacherous months.

But overall, the retirement years have been very good to both of them. They are happy and busy and full of life. The twinkle in Finney's eyes is still there. I asked him how he felt about his life now and he said simply, I am happy but I miss the people from the restaurant. The stories, the commotion, and the general business of the place were very endearing to Finney. It must have sort of felt like a newsroom in an odd sort of way. Everyone constantly running around trying to get out orders on time all while attempting to listen to each other must have hit the same sensory perception for Finney as did trying to get a news story out on time.

The smells of each place are obviously different, and the product not the same, but social gatherings are where news is discussed. And more often than not, where it is made.

Finney understands this. He relishes in it. He may be quiet and reserved but in reality he is cunning and quick. News flows in the restaurant and the pulse can be felt. The paper closes down each night but the news never stops being made. And for a true reporter like Finney, it never stops being told either.

2016 and beyond will bring new stories, new technology, and new ways of disseminating information. But one thing will always stay the same; once a journalist, always a journalist. And for our society we are so very fortunate to have someone like Finney who covered the news properly for so many years.

We are all blessed...

AFTERWARD

It has been an amazing experience in writing this book. Finney and Irene are truly local treasures. While taking on a project such as this is never easy; when one does, it can change them forever.

I had never given much thought to what it must be like to do the same job for decades and what type of person it takes to do such a thing. The dedication to ones craft is truly awe inspiring. Finney and Irene have given so much to their communities for so many years. And they still do. Even as they age, they are a constant sight about town and definitely enjoy the local restaurants.

Many of the people who live in Manchester remember them fondly. I took some time recently to take a "walk about". It's a great opportunity for a writer to feel the pulse of what people are really thinking about a subject. In the case of Finney, I wanted to reach out to some of the older residents in town and see if they remembered him. They did.

When interviewing Finney, I was taken back by his notion that no one knew about him anymore. It was sad to see someone who had done so much for a town and for so many people, become so fixed on the notion that he has been forgotten. In fact this could not be further from the truth. Even as far back as Finney's newspaper years, many people I spoke with knew of Finney and his family. He is much more highly regarded in the town than he thinks. Having The Patio restaurant with Irene has also added to his stature and memory throughout the area. Irene and Finney have employed many people in town and many young kids got their start at The Patio. There are so many people still living in town, not to mention the scores of college kids that have since moved away, all of whom Finney and Irene have touched.

Through Finney's work in creating the Globe Santa, and his years covering the news, he has touched countless other lives. My trip to the Globe has revealed an ongoing and deep felt sincerity towards Finney and all he has accomplished in his life and all he has done to give back to others.

No, this is not a man who should hold his head low and think for one moment that all he has done has somehow been forgotten. Finney and Irene still call Magnolia home. And there are many folks throughout Manchester and Magnolia who continue to hold both Irene and Finney in their hearts.

The Irene and Finney Christmas parties held at their home are an example of this. These parties are well known and looked forward to by many. Irene can still be found shuffling around the kitchen the day of the party making sure all the food is prepped and cooked to perfection. I myself have had the pleasure of watching her work during this very same day.

I feel truly blessed to have been a part of this project. Meeting Finney and Irene has truly changed both mine and my wife's lives by giving us the opportunity to self reflect on how we approach our own careers. Being able to sit with both Finney and Irene over tea on so many afternoons has also given us a greater appreciation of our own marriage and how we want our own lives to be remembered. It is not about a flashy life. This is not what makes someone great. It is about finding your passion and doing it well regardless of what it is.

Finney and Irene are respected throughout the community. And they should be. They have dedicated their lives to the service of others. The Patio restaurant helped the community in both good times and bad. Finney spent a career giving people a better understanding of what was going on in the world around them. Both of these people are gifts to the communities they live in and also to the larger collective.

Yes, they truly are remarkable people and I hope many other individuals in both Manchester and Magnolia get a chance to meet them someday. I can promise that it will be a meeting that will affect anyone who has a chance to experience it.

Thank you,

Robert Goodwin